Chronicle of Land Transport

Fiona Reynoldson

This is a reference book. You can use it to find out about the people who travelled on foot in the past. You can also use it to find out how people travelled faster in each period in history.

Contents

Using the Chronicle	2
Romans (43–410)	4
Anglo-Saxons (c. 400–1066)	6
Vikings (c. 793–1066)	8
Normans (1066–1250)	10
Late Middle Ages (c. 1250–1485)	12
Tudors (1485–1603)	14
Stuarts (1603–1714)	16
1700s (1700–1800)	18
Early 1800s (1800–c. 1830)	20
Early Victorian Times (c. 1830–1870)	22
Late Victorian Times (1870–1901)	24
Early 1900s (1901–c. 1930)	26
Mid 1900s (c. 1930–1970)	28
Glossary	30
Further Information	31
Index	32

USING THE CHRONICLE

How the Chronicles are organised

The Chronicles are organised into parts. This is because history is easier to understand if we divide it into parts called **periods**. These periods are sections of time in history.

This book has been organised into 13 periods. Each period has a starting date and an ending date. Of course, we cannot always say exactly when one period ends and another starts, so the dates are just a guide.

The choice of periods

Each of the Chronicles in the Longman Book Project covers the same 13 periods of history. To help you remember the periods, there is a special memorable event for each one shown in the top right hand corner.

Subheadings

On each page there are a number of headings and subheadings. The subheadings are the same for each period. This helps you to compare facts about transport from one period with facts about transport from another period.

The timeline

On the bottom of each page there is a timeline. The timeline stretches from Roman times to the present day. There was plenty of history **before** Roman times but it is not covered in this book.

AD | 1500

How to use the book for research

You can use the Chronicle to compare information from one period with another. For instance, you might want to compare how faster forms of transport came about in one period with how they came about in another period. If this is all you need to know, you can just read the information under these subheadings and ignore the rest of the writing.

How to use the Chronicles to cross-reference

You might want to research using more than one of the Chronicles in the Longman Book Project. You can easily do this, because each Chronicle covers the same periods in history. You can therefore compare the information in one Chronicle with that in another.

THE ROMANS 43–410

On foot – Roman legionary

Legionaries were soldiers in the Roman army. They marched and fought on foot, and to make sure that they were fit, they went on training marches several times a month. They were expected to march at about 7 kilometres per hour for at least 30 kilometres. The Roman empire was at least the size of Europe today, and the legionaries could be sent to any part of the empire to build roads, bridges and forts, and to fight.

Journeys

The legionaries not only fought and marched, they also worked as engineers and builders. The Roman army built 85,000 kilometres of roads all over the Roman empire.

Footwear

Roman legionaries wore strong leather sandals. Britain was the coldest part of the Roman empire, so the legionaries were allowed to wear sheepskin socks inside their sandals in winter.

A model of a Roman Legionary.

AD 43 – The Roman Army invades Britain.

Going faster – Roman chariots

Roman chariots were small, light carts. They had two wheels and were pulled by two or four horses.

How this came about

Chariots were used by the Chinese and the Persians a long time before the Romans. They were a widespread way of travelling quickly.

How this affected people's lives

The Romans used chariots for fast travel along the good Roman roads. For instance, letters from the emperor to his governors were sent by chariot or horse and rider.

One of the favourite sports of the Romans was chariot-racing. Huge crowds cheered on the charioteers, as teams of horses galloped at full speed around an arena for seven laps. It was a dangerous sport, but successful charioteers could earn a lot of money.

 Roman chariots.

ANGLO-SAXONS *circa 400–1066*

On foot – Shepherds

The Anglo-Saxons were skilled farmers. They planted seeds to grow wheat and other food crops. They also kept animals such as cows, pigs and sheep. Shepherds looked after all the sheep in the village.

Journeys

The sheep were always kept together in flocks, but the flocks moved about. They grazed on the hills, and they grazed on the fields after the crops had been cut in the late summer. Shepherds moved with the sheep, walking over the hills and down the valleys, looking after them all the time.

Footwear

Shepherds wore simple leather shoes, which probably had laces to fasten them like the man in the picture. Very poor shepherds would have gone barefoot.

 Poor shepherds did not wear any shoes.

AD 01　　　　　　　　　AD 500

AD 757–796 Offa digs a dyke to mark the frontier between England and Wales.

Going faster – Anglo-Saxon carts

Most Anglo-Saxons were farmers, and they needed carts to carry hay and corn from the fields to the farms, to carry wood for building, and to carry food to sell at market.

How this came about

Carts came about because the farmers wanted to clear the land to make new farms. They needed wagons to carry logs and trees. Often the soil was too heavy to dig, so the farmers used many oxen to pull their ploughs and to pull carts along the muddy roads. A few farmers used horses, but oxen were cheaper to feed than horses, so oxen usually pulled the carts and ploughs. The disadvantage was that oxen worked more slowly than horses.

How this affected people's lives

Although most Anglo-Saxons farmed the land, some earned a living by making such things as pottery. The potters needed carts to take their goods to towns, so that they could sell them. Carts were very useful.

An Anglo-Saxon cart pulled by oxen.

VIKINGS *circa 793–1066*

On foot – Viking traders

Viking traders bought and sold many different sorts of goods. They travelled on rivers and lakes as well as on roads. In summer they travelled by ship. In winter they used skates and sledges.

Journeys

The Vikings came from Scandanavia and raided Britain over and over again during this period in history. Some of the Vikings settled in Britain.

The Vikings were traders as well as raiders. They bought and sold food, fish, timber, wool, leather and furs.

Footwear

Vikings wore boots in winter. When rivers were frozen they tied skates to the bottom of the boots with leather strips. The skaters kept their feet on the ice and pushed themselves along with poles.

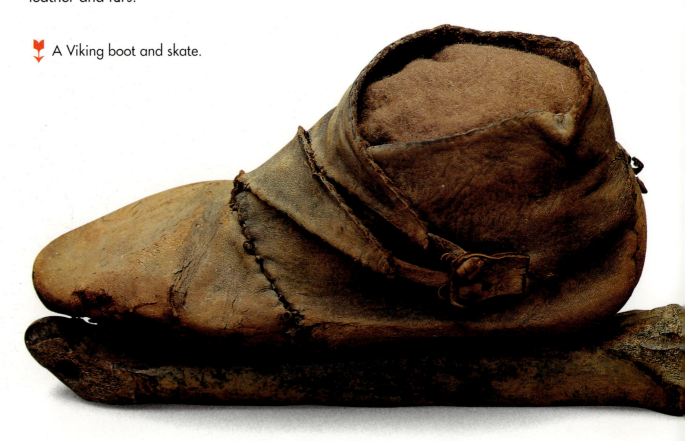

A Viking boot and skate.

AD 01   AD 500

AD 793 – The first Viking raid on Britain.

Going faster – Viking carts

Viking traders (and raiders) used ships to travel along rivers and across the sea. However, both farmers and traders used carts to travel on land. The carts were often pulled by horses.

How this came about

The Vikings travelled to many countries and saw other people using all sorts of carts, so they cut trees from their forests and made their own carts to go along the rough roads.

How this affected people's lives

In summertime, the Vikings traded with other countries, so they used carts pulled by horses or oxen to carry heavy goods to the ships. They also used carts to carry goods from one farm to another. Carts pulled by horses or oxen could carry a lot more than people could carry on their backs.

A Viking cart.

NORMANS 1066–1250

On foot – Norman archers

The Normans invaded Britain in 1066. Many Norman soldiers were archers. Once they arrived in Britain the archers travelled on foot.

Journeys

Norman archers had to march to wherever their generals told them. The archers who landed in Britain in 1066 had to march about 16 kilometres along the coast to Hastings where they camped. A few weeks later they had to march 10 kilometres north to Senlac to fight the English.

Footwear

The archers' shoes were made of leather. They were very like the Vikings' shoes, because the Normans were originally Vikings who had settled in France. The word Normans comes from 'Northmen'.

Part of the Bayeux Tapestry showing Norman archers and war-horses.

AD **1066** – The Normans won the Battle of Hastings.

Going faster – War-horses

Norman war-horses were strong but small. They had to be able to carry men who wore metal chain-mail and who used heavy lances and shields. They had to gallop as fast as they could so that they could run the enemy down.

How this came about

The rich Norman soldiers were called 'knights'. They rode small horses because no one had yet bred any big horses – all horses were much smaller than they are today.

In the next two hundred years, armour became thicker and heavier, so the Normans began to breed bigger and stronger horses.

How this affected people's lives

When the Normans had conquered England, the knights were given land to farm and many became rich and powerful men. They were ready to fight for the king and to defend their land. The knights kept horses and taught their sons to ride and fight. The horses were also used on the farms.

AD 1500   AD 2000

LATE MIDDLE AGES *circa* 1250–1485

On foot – Pilgrims

A pilgrim is a person who travels to a holy place to pray to a saint. In the Middle Ages, many people walked on pilgrimages, just as they walked everywhere else.

Journeys

In the Middle Ages pilgrims often walked hundreds of kilometres to visit the tomb of a saint in a big church or cathedral. There they prayed and asked the dead saint for his or her help. Then they had to walk home again.

Footwear

Very few drawings from the Middle Ages show exactly what people's shoes were like. Men and women all look as though they are wearing slippers! One or two manuscripts show leather boots laced up on the inside of the leg, and this sort of boot must have been worn by many men and women. As always, the very poor went barefoot.

❦ This painting shows Thomas Becket arriving in England. The people on the left hand side of the painting and the ones in the water had walked to see him arrive.

AD 1348 – The Black Death kills about one third of the people in Britain.

Going faster – Horses for rich pilgrims

Rich pilgrims rode on horseback. They often rode in large groups of ten or twenty people, so that they felt safer from attack by thieves.

How this came about

By the later Middle Ages, Britain was a more peaceful place than it had been for many hundreds of years. People felt that it was safe to travel around. Some people made money in farming or trading, and they felt they could leave their work for a while. Many pilgrims set off to visit the tombs or shrines of saints. It was a religious time, and pilgrims wanted to pray to favourite saints and to say they were sorry for things that they had done wrong.

How this affected people's lives

Rich people, who could afford horses, went on pilgrimages to Jerusalem in the Middle East. These pilgrimages took at least a year.

Many people went to shrines in Britain. Horses made it easier for them to travel to the great churches which had saints buried in them. Even so, it took days or weeks to ride along the rough tracks.

A pilgrim on horseback.

AD 1500   AD 2000

13

TUDORS   1485–1603

On foot – Farmers

In Tudor times women and men walked a great deal as part of their work. They took goods like chickens, sheep, cows, eggs and cheese to market to sell.

◂ A Tudor man walking to market.

Journeys

In Tudor times, there were farms all over Britain. Many of them were several kilometres from the nearest market town. Women set out early in the morning to walk to market carrying goods like baskets of eggs. Other women took lace or cakes or cheeses that they had made.

Footwear

Men and women who walked wore strong, leather boots.

AD 1588 – The Spanish Armada attacks the British fleet.

Going faster – Horses for the wives of rich farmers

Rich farmers had horses and their wives used the horses to ride to market. It was quicker to ride a horse, and it also meant that the farmer's wife did not have to carry heavy baskets herself.

How this came about

By Tudor times England was a fairly peaceful country. Most people obeyed the law, and thieves did not raid and steal from farms, so farmers grew lots of food. The farmers' wives looked after the chickens and cows, and they had plenty of food to spare after they had fed their families, so they loaded the spare chickens, the eggs, the butter and the cheese into baskets on horses' backs and rode off to market to sell them.

How this affected people's lives

Farmers' wives had to work hard, but they had money of their own from selling food. Country towns often had markets once a week. The main street would be crowded with cows, pigs, sheep and market stalls.

Most women and men enjoyed market days. It was a good time to buy and sell, to meet friends, and to hear the local gossip.

◀ A Tudor woman riding to market.

STUARTS 1603–1714

On foot – Ticket porters and letter carriers

In Stuart times rich people or merchants sent letters by private messengers, by ticket porters and by letter carriers.

A Stuart letter carrier.

Journeys

Ticket porters were like taxi drivers on foot. They carried letters or parcels to anywhere in the city. Letter carriers travelled over longer distances, walking from town to town.

Footwear

Letter carriers wore leather shoes or low ankle-boots. Postboys and ticket porters who rode on horses wore long leather boots which protected the lower parts of their legs and kept them warm. However, these boots were too heavy to walk in.

AD 1666 – The Great Fire of London.

Going faster – Horses for postboys

In Stuart times postboys rode on horseback. They had bags to carry letters in, and they blew on their horns to warn people to let them ride by as fast as possible.

How this came about

In Tudor times, Henry VIII had set up a postal service for the king and his government. This postal service grew very quickly. By Stuart times there were many postboys. Letters from the king or his government were sent from London to other towns. These were official letters which were about collecting taxes or about keeping the law. These letters had to be moved from place to place very quickly so the postboys used horses.

In 1660 a proper Post Office was set up for everyone to use. It was in Lombard Street in London. From then on anyone could send letters by post.

How this affected people's lives

Postboys changed peoples' lives, because merchants could send letters from London to Glasgow or from Birmingham to Bristol very quickly, so business and trade grew. However, it cost as much as a day's pay to send a letter a long way, so only businessmen and rich people sent letters.

 A Stuart postboy on his horse.

1700s 1700–1800

On foot – Walking in towns

On foot – Walking in towns

By the 1700s the roads in towns and cities were often paved with cobbles. This stopped the roads from being muddy, but they were still dirty from the droppings of all the animals in the towns. Most people still walked when they went on short journeys in town.

Journeys

Fruit sellers, like the one in the picture, pushed barrows of fruit to the market. Farmers drove cows and sheep from the country to sell in the city.

Footwear

In the 1700s, rich people wore smart shoes with buckles. Sometimes the shoes were even made of silk or of very soft leather.

Ordinary people wore heavy leather boots with nails studding the heels and soles. These came to be known as hobnailed boots.

A London street in the 1700s.

AD 1776 – The Americans declare their independence from Britain.

Going faster – Horses and carriages

By the 1700s, horses were used more and more. They were ridden and they pulled carts and carriages. A cart with a heavy load moved at about 3 km/h. On a good road, a light carriage pulled by two fast horses could travel at 24 km/h.

How this came about

At this time there were many more carts and horses on the roads than at any time before. In the 1700s the number of people living in Britain doubled. More people meant that more food was needed. More carts brought food and other goods to the cities.

How it affected people's lives

More people started to travel and more people had horses in the 1700s. Some rich, clever farmers thought of new food crops to grow like turnips. They also learnt how to breed bigger and more woolly sheep. Other farmers all over Britain heard about this. Some of them got on their horses and rode many kilometres to find out about these new ways. Other men set up factories to make woollen cloth for clothes. They wanted to send their cloth on pack horses or in carts to the cities, which were becoming bigger and bigger.

EARLY 1800s 1800–*circa* 1830

On foot – Drovers

Drovers drove animals to markets. The drovers' roads were often tracks of grass or sand which wound across the country. The drovers avoided the main roads because their herds of animals walked slowly and blocked the roads.

Footwear

Drovers had good leather lace up boots because they spent so much time walking.

Journeys

Many drovers' roads started in Scotland and Wales. They snaked across the hills and into England for several hundred miles. There were big markets in London where thousands of animals were sold. As the drovers neared London they often had to use the main roads to go into the city. They were unpopular with other road-users such as people in carts, carriages and stagecoaches, because they blocked the roads.

A drover with his dog.

AD 1815 – The Battle of Waterloo.

Going faster – Stagecoaches

Stagecoaches were like long distance buses. They were pulled by four horses and could travel at about 11 or 12 km/h. The de luxe or best coaches were the Royal Mail ones, which carried the letters and parcels for the Post Office, and took a few passengers too.

How this came about

Stagecoaches came about because more people wanted to travel. New, stone roads were built between the main cities by engineers like Telford and Macadam, so that the heavy stagecoaches could run smoothly.

How this affected people's lives

Fast coaches affected peoples' lives because letters and parcels went quickly to all cities and towns in Britain. This helped businesses of all sorts. People were now able to travel to work or to see their friends. The sort of people who travelled on stagecoaches were governesses, engineers, farmers and shopkeepers.

 This stagecoach carried passengers as well as the Royal Mail.

EARLY VICTORIAN TIMES *circa* 1830–1870

On foot – Farm-workers

Although the cities were growing in mid-Victorian times, most people still worked in the country. All over the countryside, fields had to be ploughed every winter so that farmers could sow seed to produce wheat and other crops.

Journeys

Ploughmen walked many kilometres every day up and down the fields behind teams of horses which pulled the ploughs.

Footwear

Farm-workers often wore leather ankle boots called 'high-lows'. Sometimes they wore leather gaiters which strapped round their legs below the knee. The gaiters stopped the ploughman's trousers from getting muddy and wet.

 A farmer talking to his ploughmen.

AD **1851** – The Great Exhibition took place in London.

Going faster – Trains

Railway trains were a new form of transport. They could go much faster than horses. However, horses were still needed to pull carts from the farms to the stations and back again.

How this came about

In the early 1800s engineers like George Stephenson had made steam engines that could turn wheels. Soon steam locomotives were pulling trains along railway lines. By early Victorian times, railway lines were being built all over Britain. Long distance stagecoaches were dying out. Travellers preferred to go by train. They used horses or the newly invented bicycles to travel short distances.

How this affected people's lives

Trains meant that people could travel quickly all over Britain. They could travel from 80 to 110 km/h, or even faster. People could get to work quickly; they could go on holiday to the seaside; and they could travel to visit their families. Food that goes off quickly, like milk or strawberries, could be sent quickly from the country to towns on trains.

 Loading strawberries on to a train going to London.

LATE VICTORIAN TIMES 1870–1901

On foot – Women farm-workers

Women as well as men had always worked on farms. In late Victorian times they did many jobs. Women farm-workers helped to get the harvest in by raking up the wheat and making it into bundles. They picked fruits, they hoed vegetables and they did the back-breaking work of picking up stones from the fields and digging up potatoes. All these jobs were done on foot.

Journeys

Women farm-workers walked to work across the fields and along the country lanes. They had to work long hours in the fields and then to walk a long way back home in the evenings.

Footwear

Women wore ankle-boots like men. Often they were fastened with laces. In some parts of Britain, women wore wooden clogs, or leather clogs with thick wooden soles.

 Women walking home after a day's work in the fields.

AD 1871 – The beginning of free education for all children.

Going faster – Bicycles

Bicycles were a popular form of transport in late Victorian times. They were common in towns and in the country. Many people could afford bicycles and they made it easier to get around.

How this came about

Bicycles were invented in mid Victorian times but, until later in that century, they were very expensive.

Rubber tyres filled with air were invented in Scotland in 1888. This meant that bicycles were much more comfortable, although many still did not have brakes.

How this affected people's lives

As bicycles became cheaper and more comfortable, people began to ride them for pleasure. Many cycling clubs were set up all over Britain.

In the 1890s the frames of bicycles were changed so that women in their long skirts would find it easier to get onto the saddle.

A woman getting on one of the first bicycles.

25

EARLY 1900s   1901–*circa* 1930s

On foot – Soldiers of the First World War

The First World War started in 1914: Britain, France and Russia went to war against Germany and Austria. The war was fought in several parts of the world, sometimes on sandy beaches and sometimes in muddy fields. Many of the British soldiers fought in France. Most of them had to march into battle and fought the war on foot.

Journeys

Millions of soldiers fought in the war. To reach the battlefields, British soldiers travelled by train and then marched from railway stations along the dusty French roads.

Footwear

The soldiers wore leather lace-up boots with nails on the soles and heels. The marching soldiers made little noise on the sandy roads, but the nails made a ringing sound as they marched over the cobbled stone streets of the small French towns. The soldiers wound strips of canvas, called 'puttees', round their lower legs. This helped to keep their trousers clean.

 Scottish soldiers marching in France.

AD 1928 – Everyone over 21 years old is given the vote.

Going faster – Tanks

Tanks are large metal boxes which run on caterpillar tracks. They have guns mounted on them. Men sit inside them to drive them and to fire the guns. The name 'tank' was used because the metal boxes looked like water tanks.

How this came about

By the time of the First World War, men could make guns that fired bullets very fast. They were called 'machine guns'. These guns made life very dangerous for soldiers on foot. Soldiers who survived the machine guns often got caught on barbed wire which had been laid down by the enemy. So British inventors thought of making a large, moving, metal box which could drive over the barbed wire. Men could sit inside the metal box and drive it towards the enemy, shooting as they went.

How this affected people's lives

Tanks saved lives because the soldiers inside them were protected from the guns and the barbed wire. Tanks helped to win the war for Britain, but there were problems with them. One problem was that they often got stuck if the ground was muddy, and then it was easy for the enemy to blow them up.

The tank's caterpillar tracks helped it to move on all surfaces.

MID 1900s *circa* 1930–1970

On foot – Walking for fun

Large numbers of people walked for fun in the mid 1900s. They liked to get out of the towns and to walk in the countryside away from the busy roads.

Journeys

Some people went on walking holidays. They walked along footpaths and old tracks. They often stayed overnight in Youth Hostels. Other people just went for day-long walks. This was called rambling.

Footwear

In the mid 1900s, walking boots were still made of leather and were laced up. By the 1970s, trainers made of light leather or fabric with thick rubber soles were becoming more popular.

 Walkers in the 1930s.

AD 1948 – The National Health Service was set up.

Going faster – Motor-cars

The motor-car was invented in late Victorian times. Between the 1930s and the 1970s many people bought cars.

How this came about

During the 1900s factories were set up to make cars. These factories produced cars more cheaply so the price came down. More people could afford the cars.

By the 1970s, ordinary people earned far more money than a Roman legionary, or a farm-worker in Victorian times, would ever have dreamed of earning. So ordinary people could afford to buy and run cars.

How this affected people's lives

For nearly 2000 years most people had walked wherever they wanted to go. Only rich people could afford to go by horse. However by the 1970s, lots of ordinary people could afford to buy a car. More roads had to be built as more people travelled all over Britain for their work or for their holidays.

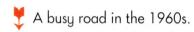
A busy road in the 1960s.

GLOSSARY

Charioteers — Charioteers were people who drove chariots.

Circa — Circa means about, or around. It is used when we are not sure about exact dates.

Clogs — Clogs are heavy wooden shoes.

Drovers — Drovers were people who drove cattle along the road to market, where they would be sold.

Emperor — An Emperor is someone who rules an Empire just as a King rules a country.

Engineers — Engineers are people who make or work with engines.

Governor — A governor was someone who ruled part of the Roman Empire for the Emperor.

Licences — A licence is the right, or gives permission to do something.

Manufacturers — Manufacturers are people who make things.

Manuscripts — A manuscript is a book or document written by hand.

Market town — A market town is a town where a market is held for the buying and selling of goods.

Pilgrimages — A pilgrimage is a journey to a holy place.

Rutted — Rutted roads are roads with deep marks made by wheels.

Scandinavia — In Viking times, Scandinavia was made up from Norway Sweden, Denmark and Iceland.

Shrines — A shrine is a holy place such as the tomb of a saint.

Youth hostels — Youth hostels are places where people can stay overnight. They don't charge a lot of money.

FURTHER INFORMATION

Books

Look at books about the different times in history.

Ancient Rome by Simon James, Dorling Kindersley 1990
Look at the contents to find chapters on 'A Day at the Races' and 'Transport, Travel and Trade'.

Horse – Dorling Kindersley 1992
Look at sections such as 'War Horse' and 'Horsepower'.

Museums

The London Transport Museum
Open: 7 days a week, 10.00 a.m. to 6.00 p.m.

Northampton Museum and Art Galleries
Open: Monday to Saturday, 10.00 a.m. to 5.00 p.m. and Sunday 2.00 p.m. to 5.00 p.m. Admission free.
This museum contains the largest book and shoe collection in Europe, from Romans to present day.

INDEX

Aa archers 10

Bb Battle of Hastings 10, 11
Bayeux tapestry 10
bicycles 25
books 12, 14, 16, 18, 20, 22, 24, 26, 28

Cc cars 29
carts 7, 9, 10
chariots 5
coaches 21
clogs 24

Dd drovers 20

Ff farmers 6, 7, 14, 15, 19, 23
farm horses 22, 23, 24

Gg gaiters 22

Hh horses 7, 9, 11, 13, 15, 19, 23

Kk knights 11

Ll Legionary 4
letter carriers 16

Mm messengers 16

Nn Normans 10, 11

Oo oxen 7, 9

Pp pilgrims 12, 13
post boys 16, 17

Rr railways 25

Ss sandals 4
shepherds 6
shoes 6, 10, 10, 12, 16, 18
skates 8
soldiers 4, 26
stagecoaches 22

Tt tanks 27
ticket porters 16
traders 8, 9
trainers 28
trains 25

Ww walking 18, 28
war horses 11